D1449461

Transition Guide to

Microsoft® Office 2007

PEARSON

Prentice Hall

Upper Saddle River, New Jersey 07458

10 9 8 7 6 5 4 3 2 1
ISBN 0-13-159363-3

CONTENTS

Introduction

Explore the new features of Microsoft® Office 2007!

Microsoft® Office 2007 introduces many new features to help you get your work done more efficiently and effectively. By far the biggest change in Office 2007 is the new user interface. A user interface, which is what you see on the screen when you are using software, provides a way for you to interact with software and tell it what tasks you want to perform. With Office 2007, Microsoft has streamlined the user interface, so that you can more quickly and easily locate program features and complete tasks.

The most noticeable user interface change in Office 2007 is the replacement of the traditional menus and toolbars with the **Ribbon**, which groups commands in a way that corresponds directly to the way people work. The Ribbon works along with **galleries** and the **Live Preview** feature to present you with graphical examples of formatting results, to help eliminate the time wasted on trial and error. The **KeyTips** feature allows users to invoke commands with just a few simple steps.

This Transition Guide to Microsoft® Office 2007 is designed to:

- Introduce you to the new Office 2007 user interface components.
- Demonstrate—using a side-by-side comparison with Office 2003—how to perform basic tasks and use the new features that are shared across the Office 2007 programs.

Learning how to perform these basic tasks right up front will put you on your way to producing professional-looking documents, effective spreadsheets, compelling presentations, and powerful databases using Microsoft Office 2007.

Identifying Common Interface Components

As previously noted, a user interface provides the means of communication between you and a software program. In Microsoft® Office 2007, the primary software programs—Word, Excel, PowerPoint, and Access—all share common user interface components.

Common User Interface Components	Description
Office button	Displays the Office menu, which contains a list of commands related to things you can do with a document, such as opening, saving, printing, or sharing.
Quick Access Toolbar (QAT)	Displays buttons to perform frequently used commands, such as Save, Undo, and Redo, with a single click. For commands that you use frequently, you can add additional buttons to the Quick Access Toolbar.
Mini toolbar	Provides quick access to the most frequently used formatting commands specific to the context of the selected text.
Ribbon	Organizes commands on tabs and then groups the commands by topic for performing related document tasks.
Status bar	Displays the page and line number, word count, and the Proof button on the left side. On the right side, displays buttons to control the look of the window. The status bar can be customized to include other information.

The top of the program window contains the **Office button** that, when clicked, displays the Office menu. The Office menu contains a list of things you can do with a document—such as opening, saving, printing, or sharing. The **Quick Access Toolbar (QAT)**—also at the top of the program window—provides access to commonly used commands, such as Save, Undo, and Redo.

The primary command center is the **Ribbon**. Displaying as a strip across the top of the program window, the Ribbon contains tabs that are organized around the major tasks relevant to each of the programs. Each tab contains groups of related visual commands.

The **Mini toolbar** which appears when text is selected provides access to formatting commands specific to selected text. The bottom of the window contains a **status bar** that gives general information, view options, and the Zoom slider.

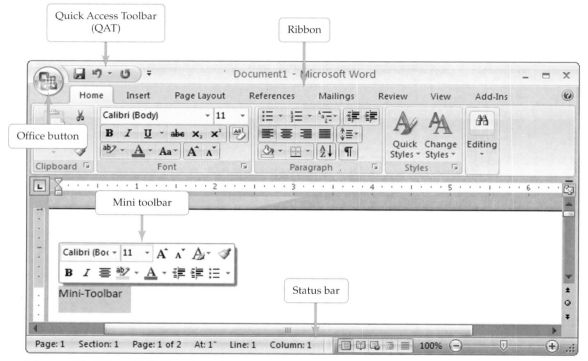

Microsoft® Office 2007 User Interface Elements

The Ribbon, Groups, Galleries, and Dialog Box Launchers

On the Ribbon, the tabs containing groups of basic and commonly used commands are always available. On the Word Ribbon, for example, you will find tabs for Home, Insert, Page Layout, References, Mailings, Review, View, and Add-Ins.

Each Ribbon tab contains several **groups** of related commands. The Word 2007 Home tab, for example, includes groups such as Font, Paragraph, and Editing, each of which includes buttons and options related to similar tasks. In the lower-right corner of a group, a dialog box launcher may display. Clicking a dialog box launcher opens a dialog box or task pane related to that group. Clicking the Font dialog box launcher, for example, opens the Font dialog box.

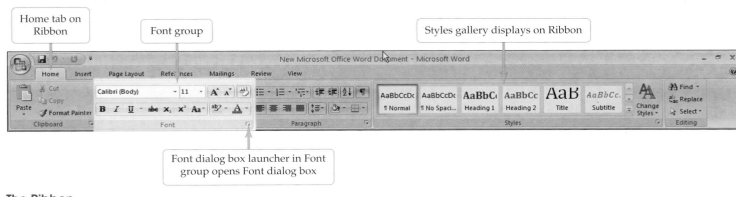

Home tab on Ribbon

Font group

Styles gallery displays on Ribbon

Font dialog box launcher in Font group opens Font dialog box

The Ribbon

A **gallery** is a set of options that display as thumbnails or graphics. Galleries provide you with a set of visual results from which to choose when you are working on a document. Galleries display in many places in the Office 2007 user interface. For example, as shown in the figure on page 7, the Home tab has an in-Ribbon gallery to show different text-formatting options. Other galleries display when you click a button on the Ribbon. For example, to display the WordArt gallery, click the Insert tab, and in the Text group, click the WordArt button.

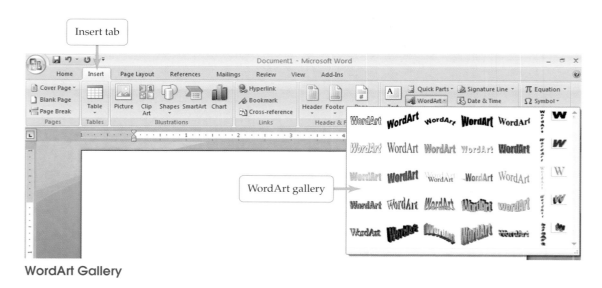

WordArt Gallery

Live Preview

Whenever you hover over a formatting option with your mouse, Office 2007 instantly shows you how the change will impact your document. For example, as you point to a style in the Styles gallery or a font in the Font list, Word responds by showing you a preview of how your document will look if selected. Live Preview is designed to stop the frustrating cycle of clicking and then undoing changes to get just the right format. With Live Preview, you can pick before you click.

The Mini Toolbar

The Mini toolbar displays automatically when you select text in a document. The Mini toolbar is designed to provide quick access to common formatting commands, such as Bold, Italic, Bullets and Numbering, and more.

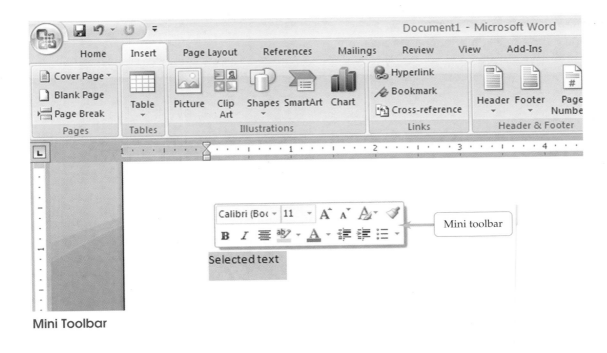

Mini Toolbar

The Quick Access Toolbar

The Quick Access Toolbar, which displays in the upper-left corner of the program window, provides quick access to frequently used commands such as Save, Undo, and Redo. The Customize Quick Access Toolbar menu enables you to add more buttons to the toolbar, so you can put your favorite commands within easy reach. The menu also contains an option to minimize the Ribbon to make more space available on the screen.

Quick Access Toolbar

Customize Quick Access Toolbar menu

Minimize the Ribbon command

Quick Access Toolbar

KeyTips

In addition to supporting standard keyboard shortcuts (for example, CTRL+B to bold text), Office 2007 supports a new type of keyboard shortcut, called KeyTips. To activate KeyTips, press ALT or the F10 function key on the keyboard. Small yellow KeyTips will display on the Ribbon and Quick Access Toolbar, with each tab on the Ribbon represented by a letter, and each button on the Quick Access Toolbar represented by a number. Pressing the letter N, for example, will select the Insert tab; you can then select a specific command by pressing its KeyTip. *Note:* Some KeyTips consist of two characters instead of one.

KeyTips on Office button and Quick Access Toolbar

KeyTips on Ribbon tabs

KeyTips

Completing Basic Tasks

Opening a File

1. Click File on the menu bar.
2. From the File menu, click Open.

1. Click the Office button.
2. From the Office menu, click Open.

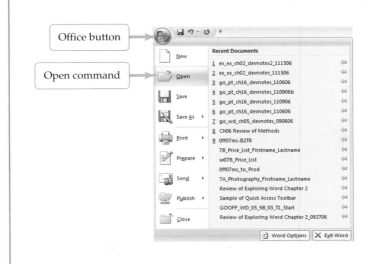

Office button

Open command

Other Ways:

- Click the Open button on the Standard toolbar.
- Press CTRL+O.
- Press ALT+F, O.

Other Ways:

- Press CTRL+O.
- Press ALT+F, O.

Microsoft® Office 2003

1. Click File on the menu bar.
2. From the File menu, click Close.

Microsoft® Office 2007

1. Click the Office button.
2. From the Office menu, click Close.

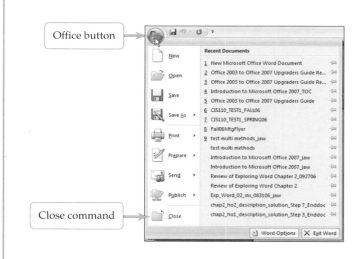

Office button

Close command

Other Ways:

- Click the Close button on the title bar.
- Press ALT+F, C.

Other Ways:

- Double-click the Office button. *Note:* If no other documents are open, double-clicking the Office button will also close the program.
- Press ALT+F, C.

Saving a File with the Same File Name

Microsoft® Office 2003

1. Click File on the menu bar.
2. From the File menu, click Save.

Microsoft® Office 2007

1. Click the Office button.
2. From the Office menu, click Save.

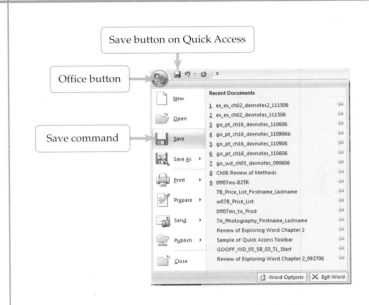

Other Ways:

- Click the Save button on the Standard toolbar.
- Press CTRL+S.
- Press ALT+F, S.

Other Ways:

- Click the Save button on the Quick Access Toolbar.
- Press ALT+1.
- Press CTRL+S.
- Press ALT+F, S.

Microsoft® Office 2003

1. Click File on the menu bar.
2. From the File menu, click Save As.

Microsoft® Office 2007

1. Click the Office button.
2. From the Office menu, click Save As.

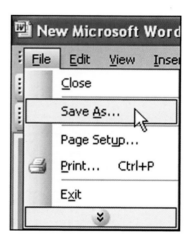

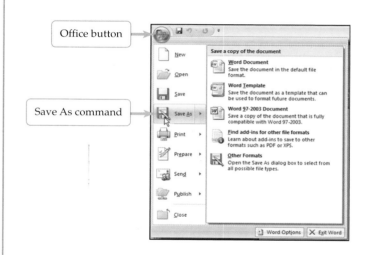

Other Ways:

- Press F12.
- Press ALT+F, A.

Other Ways:

- Press F12.
- Press ALT+F, A.

Microsoft® Office 2003

1. Click File on the menu bar.
2. From the File menu, click Properties.

Microsoft® Office 2007

1. Click the Office button.
2. From the Office menu, point to Prepare, and then click Properties. The Document Information Panel displays.

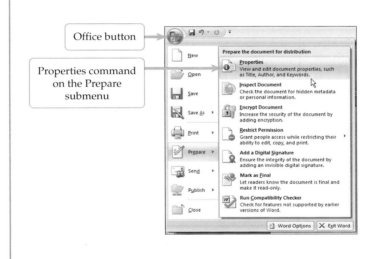

Office button

Properties command on the Prepare submenu

Other Ways:

- Press ALT+F, I.

Other Ways:

- Press ALT+F, E, P.

Microsoft® Office 2003

1. Click File on the menu bar.
2. From the File menu, click Print or Print Preview (or click the Print button on the Standard toolbar). *Note:* Clicking the Print button sends one copy of the file to the default printer.

Microsoft® Office 2007

1. Click the Office button.
2. From the Office menu, point to Print, and then click Print, Quick Print, or Print Preview (or just click Print from the Office menu to open the Print dialog box). *Note:* The Quick Print command sends one copy of the file to the default printer.

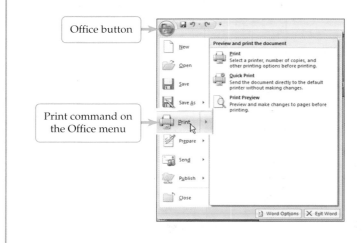

Other Ways:

- Press CTRL+P or ALT+F, P to open the Print dialog box.
- Press ALT+F, V to open the Print Preview window.

Other Ways:

- Press CTRL+P or ALT+F, P or ALT+F, W, P to open the Print dialog box.
- Press ALT+F, W, Q to do a Quick Print or ALT+F, W, V to open the Print Preview window.

Editing and Formatting Documents

Moving or Copying Text

Microsoft® Office 2003

1. Click Edit on the menu bar.
2. From the Edit menu, click Cut or Copy.

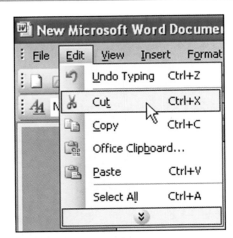

Microsoft® Office 2007

1. On the Home tab, in the Clipboard group, click the Cut button or the Copy button.

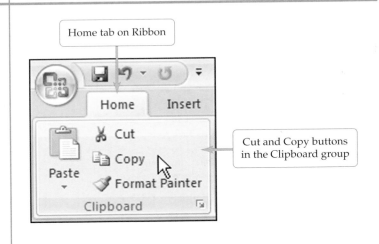

Home tab on Ribbon

Cut and Copy buttons in the Clipboard group

Other Ways:

Cut
- Click the Cut button on the Standard toolbar.
- Press CTRL+X.
- Right-click the selected text and then click Cut on the shortcut menu.

Copy
- Click the Copy button on the Standard toolbar.
- Press CTRL+C.
- Right-click the selected text and then click Copy on the shortcut menu.

Other Ways:

Cut
- Press ALT+H, X.
- Press CTRL+X.
- Right-click the selected text and then click Cut on the shortcut menu.

Copy
- Press ALT+H, C.
- Press CTRL+C.
- Right-click the selected text and then click Copy on the shortcut menu.

Microsoft® Office 2003

1. Click Edit on the menu bar.
2. From the Edit menu, click Find, Replace, or Go To.

Microsoft® Office 2007

Find and Go To
1. On the Home tab, in the Editing group, click the Find button arrow.
2. Click the Find or Go To command.

Replace
1. On the Home tab, in the Editing group, click the Replace button.

Find arrow in Editing group displays the Find and Go To commands

Find and Replace buttons in the Editing group

Other Ways:

Find
- Press CTRL+F.
- Press ALT+E, F.
- Click the Select Browse Object button on the vertical scroll bar and then click the Find button.

Replace
- Press CTRL+H.
- Click the Select Browse Object button on the vertical scroll bar, click the Find button, and then click the Replace tab.
- Press ALT+E, E.

Go To
- Press CTRL+G.
- Click the Select Browse Object button on the vertical scroll bar, and then click the Go To button.
- Press ALT+E, G.

Other Ways:

Find
- On the Home tab, in the Editing group, click the Find button.
- Press CTRL+F.
- Press ALT+H, FD, F.
- Click the Select Browse Object button on the vertical scroll bar and then click the Find button.

Replace
- Press CTRL+H.
- Click the Select Browse Object button on the vertical scroll bar, click the Find button, and then click the Replace tab.
- Press ALT+H, FD, G.

Go To
- Press CTRL+G.
- Click the Select Browse Object button on the vertical scroll bar, and then click the Go To button.
- Press ALT+H, R.

Microsoft® Office 2003

1. Click the Undo button or the Redo button on the Standard toolbar.

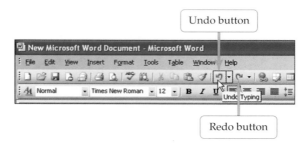

Undo button

Redo button

Microsoft® Office 2007

1. Click the Undo button or the Redo button on the Quick Access Toolbar.

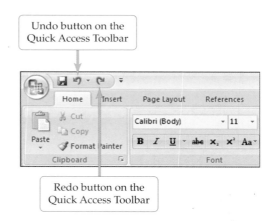

Undo button on the Quick Access Toolbar

Redo button on the Quick Access Toolbar

Other Ways:

- Click Edit on the menu bar, and then from the Edit menu, click Undo or Redo.
- Press CTRL+Z to undo or CTRL+Y to redo.

Other Ways:

- Press ALT+2 to undo or ALT+3 to redo.
- Press CTRL+Z to undo or CTRL+Y to redo.

Microsoft® Office 2003

Bold, Italic, Underline

- Click the Bold button, the Italic button, or the Underline button on the Formatting toolbar.

Font, Font Size, Font Color

- Click the Font arrow, the Font Size arrow, or the Font Color arrow on the Formatting toolbar.

Microsoft® Office 2007

Bold, Italic, Underline

- On the Home tab, in the Font group, click the Bold button, the Italic button, or the Underline button.

Font, Font Size, Font Color

- On the Home tab, in the Font group, click the Font arrow, the Font Size arrow, or the Font Color arrow.

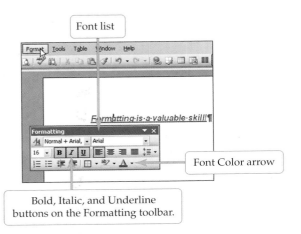

Font list

Font Color arrow

Bold, Italic, and Underline
buttons on the Formatting toolbar.

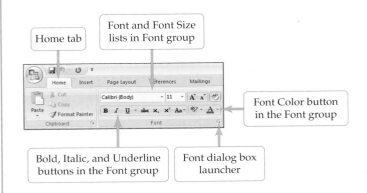

Home tab

Font and Font Size
lists in Font group

Font Color button
in the Font group

Bold, Italic, and Underline
buttons in the Font group

Font dialog box
launcher

Other Ways:

Bold, Italic, Underline
- Click the Format menu, and then from the Format menu, click Font.
- Press ALT+F,O or CTRL+D to open the Font dialog box.
- Right-click, and then from the shortcut menu, click Font.
- Press CTRL+B to bold, CTRL+I to italicize, or CTRL+U to underline.

Font, Font Size, Font Color
- Click the Format menu, and then from the Format menu, click Font.
- Press ALT+F,O or CTRL+D to open the Font dialog box.
- Right-click, and then click Font from the shortcut menu.
- Press CTRL+SHIFT+F to change the font or CTRL+SHIFT+P to change the font size.

Other Ways:

Bold, Italic, Underline
- Click the Font dialog box launcher (or press CTRL+D) to open the Font dialog box. With the text selected, click the Bold or Italic button on the Mini toolbar.
- Right-click, and then from the shortcut menu, click Font.
- Press CTRL+B (or ALT+H, 1) to bold, CTRL+I (or ALT+H, 2) to italicize, or CTRL+U (or ALT+H, 3) to underline.

Font, Font Size, Font Color
- Click the Font dialog box launcher (or press CTRL+D) to open the Font dialog box.
- Select text and then click the Font, Font Size, or Font Color arrow on the Mini toolbar.
- Right-click, and then click Font from the shortcut menu.
- Press CTRL+SHIFT+F (or ALT+H, FF) to change the font, CTRL+SHIFT+P (or ALT+H, FS) to change the font size, or ALT+H, FC to change the font color.

Copying Formats with Format Painter

Microsoft® Office 2003	Microsoft® Office 2007
1. Select text with the format to copy and then click the Format Painter button on the Standard toolbar. 2. Select the text to apply the format.	1. Select text with the format to copy, and then on the Home tab, in the Clipboard group, click the Format Painter button. 2. Select the text to apply the format.

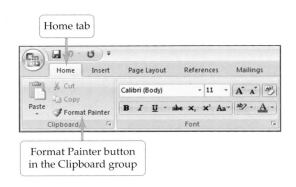

Home tab

Format Painter button in the Clipboard group

Other Ways:

- Select text with the format to be copied. To copy formatting to more than one block of text, double-click Format Painter. Select the series of text items to apply the format.

Other Ways:

- Select text with the format to copy, and then click the Format Painter button on the Mini toolbar. Select the text to apply the format.
- Select text with the format to copy, and then press CTRL+SHIFT+C. Select the text to apply the format.
- Select text with the format to copy, and then press ALT+H, F, P. Select the text to apply the format.
- Select text with the format to copy. To copy formatting to more than one block of text, double-click Format Painter. Select the series of text items to apply the format.

Using Proofing and Language Tools

Using Proofing Tools

<table>
<tr><td>

Microsoft® Office 2003

Spelling and Grammar
- Click Tools on the menu bar and then click Spelling and Grammar.

Research
- Click Tools on the menu bar and then click Research.

Thesaurus
- Click Tools on the menu bar, point to Language, and then click Thesaurus on the Language menu.

Translate
- Click Tools on the menu bar, point to Language, and then click Translate on the Language menu.

</td><td>

Microsoft® Office 2007

Spelling and Grammar
- Click the Review tab, and then in the Proofing group, click the Spelling & Grammar button.

Research
- Click the Review tab, and then in the Proofing group, click the Research button.

Thesaurus
- Click the Review tab, and then in the Proofing group, click the Thesaurus button.

Translate
- Click the Review tab, and then in the Proofing group, click the Translate button.

</td></tr>
</table>

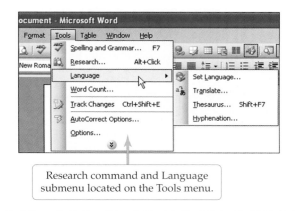

Research command and Language submenu located on the Tools menu.

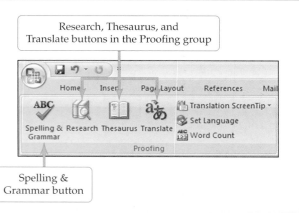

Research, Thesaurus, and Translate buttons in the Proofing group

Spelling & Grammar button

Spelling and Grammar
- Click the Spelling button on the Standard toolbar.
- Press F7 or ALT+T, S to open the Spelling and Grammar dialog box.
- Right-click the misspelled word, and then click the correct spelling in the list.
- Right-click the misspelled word, and then click Spelling to open the Spelling and Grammar dialog box.

Research
- Press ALT+CLICK or press ALT+T, R to open the Research task pane.
- Right-click the term, and then click Look Up on the shortcut menu.

Thesaurus
- Select and word, and then press SHIFT+F7 or press ALT+T, L, T to open the Thesaurus.
- Right-click a word, and then click Synonyms on the shortcut menu. Select a synonym from the displayed list or click Thesaurus.

Translate
- Select a word, and then press ALT+T, L, A to use the Translation options.
- Right-click a word or sentence, and then click Translate from the shortcut menu.

Other Ways:

Spelling and Grammar
- Press F7 or ALT+R, S to open the Spelling and Grammar dialog box.
- Right-click the misspelled word, and then click the correct spelling in the list.
- Right-click the misspelled word, and then click Spelling to open the Spelling and Grammar dialog box.

Research
- Press ALT+CLICK or press ALT+R, R to open the Research task pane.
- Right-click the term, and then click Look Up on the shortcut menu.

Thesaurus
- Press SHIFT+F7 or press ALT+R, E to open the Thesaurus.
- Right-click a word, and then click Synonyms from the shortcut menu. Select a synonym from the displayed list or click Thesaurus.

Translate
- Press ALT+R, L to use the Translation options.
- Right-click a word or sentence, and then click Translate from the shortcut menu.

Microsoft® Office 2003

1. Click Tools on the menu bar.
2. From the Tools menu, click AutoCorrect Options.

Microsoft® Office 2007

1. Click the Office button.
2. In the Office menu window, click the Word Options button.
3. In the left pane, click Proofing.
4. In the Proofing window, click the AutoCorrect Options button.

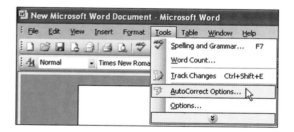

Word Options button in the Office menu window

AutoCorrect Options button

Other Ways:

- Press ALT+T, A.
- Click Insert on the menu bar, then from the Insert menu, click AutoText two times. In the AutoCorrect dialog box, click the AutoCorrect tab.
- Press ALT+I, A, X, and then press CTRL+TAB to select the AutoCorrect tab.

Other Ways:

- Press ALT+F, I. Press DOWN ARROW to select Proofing, and then press ALT+A.

Viewing Documents

Using Zoom

Microsoft® Office 2003

1. Click View on the menu bar.
2. From the View menu, click Zoom.

Microsoft® Office 2007

1. On the View tab, in the Zoom group, click the Zoom button.
2. In the Zoom dialog box, set the Zoom level, and then click the OK button.

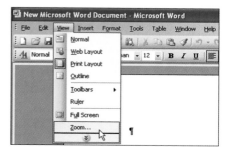

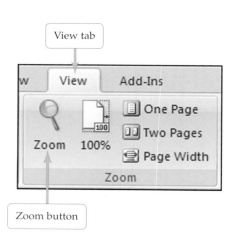

- On the Standard toolbar, click the Zoom button arrow, and then select a Zoom percentage.
- Press ALT+V, Z to open the Zoom dialog box, select a Zoom option, and then click the OK button.
- On the Standard toolbar, type a zoom percentage in the Zoom box.

- On the View tab, in the Zoom group, click one of the following buttons: 100%, Page, Two Pages, or Page Width.
- Press ALT+M, Q to open the Zoom dialog box, select a Zoom option, and then click the OK button.
- On the status bar, click the Zoom level button to open the Zoom dialog box, select a Zoom option, and then click the OK button.
- Drag the Zoom slider to the left to zoom out or to the right to zoom in.
- On the Zoom slider, click the Zoom Out or the Zoom In button.

Microsoft® Office 2003

1. Click View on the menu bar.
2. From the View menu, click Normal, Web Layout, Print Layout, Reading Layout, or Outline.

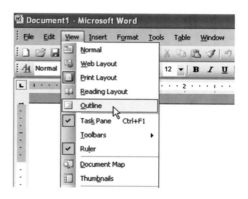

Other Ways:

- Press ALT+V, N (or W, P, R, O) to change the view.
- On the status bar, click one of the following buttons: Normal View, Web Layout View, Print Layout View, Outline View or Reading Layout.

Microsoft® Office 2007

1. On the View tab, in the Document Views group, click one of the following buttons: Print Layout, Full Screen Reading, Web Layout, Outline, or Draft.

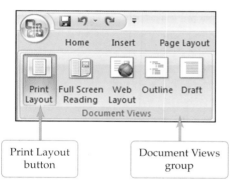

Print Layout button

Document Views group

Other Ways:

- Press ALT+V, P (or F, L, U or E) to change the view.
- On the status bar, click one of the following buttons: Print Layout, Full Screen Reading, Web Layout, Outline or Draft.

Using Online Help

Microsoft® Office 2003

1. Click Help on the menu bar.
2. From the Help menu, click Microsoft Office Word Help.

Microsoft® Office 2007

1. In the upper right corner of the Ribbon, click the Microsoft Office Help button.
2. Type a term in the Search text box and then click the Search button.

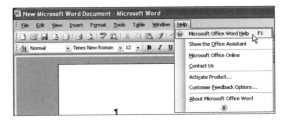

Search text box

Search button

Other Ways:

- Press F1.
- In a dialog box, in the upper right corner, click the Help button to get suggested help relevant to the commands in the dialog box.
- Click Help on the menu bar. From the Help menu, click Show the Office Assistant or Microsoft Office Online.
- In the Type a Question for Help box, type a search term, and then press ENTER.
- Click the Microsoft Office Help button on the Standard toolbar.

Other Ways:

- Press F1.
- In a dialog box, in the upper right corner, click the Help button to get suggested help relevant to the commands in the dialog box.